Minim Guide

Guide to Organizing and Decluttering Your Home Based on Principles of Minimalism to Live an Intentional Life With More Time And Less Stress

By Eugene Levins

© **Copyright 2020 - All rights reserved.**

The content contained within this book may not be reproduced, duplicated or transmitted without direct written permission from the author or the publisher.

Under no circumstances will any blame or legal responsibility be held against the publisher or author for any damages, reparation, or monetary loss due to the information contained within this book. Either directly or indirectly.

Legal Notice:

This book is copyright protected. This book is only for personal use. You cannot amend, distribute, sell, use, quote or paraphrase any part, or the content within this book, without the consent of the author or publisher.

Disclaimer Notice:

Please note the information contained within this document is for educational and entertainment purposes only. All effort has been executed to present accurate, up to date and reliable, complete information. No warranties of any kind are declared or implied. Readers acknowledge that the author is not engaging in the rendering of legal, financial, medical or professional advice. The content within this book has been derived from various sources. Please consult a licensed professional before attempting any techniques outlined in this book.

By reading this document, the reader agrees that under no circumstances is the author responsible for any losses, direct or indirect, which are incurred as a result of the use of information contained within this document, including, but not limited to, —errors, omissions, or inaccuracies.

Contents

Introduction 1

Chapter 1: You Do Not Need to Be Bogged Down with "Stuff." 5

    Bringing Minimal Design Into Your Home 6

    Minimalism as a Response to Materialism 9

Chapter 2: The Initial steps to a Minimalistic Way of life 13

    Decrease Your Clutter 14

    Get rid of Boxes 16

    Dealing with Cables 18

    One In, One Out 18

    Removing Things 19

Chapter 3: Take Pleasure In the Liberty that a Minimalistic Way of life can Offer 22

    Producing a Zen Area 23

    You Don't Need to Clean as Much! 25

    Financial Freedom 27

Chapter 4: Increasing Your Productivity with a Minimalist Way of life .. 30

    The Ultimate Office 31

    Keeping Your Tech Fast and Clean 36

Chapter 5: Include the Crucial Things 38

    Turning Your House Into an Asset 40

    How to Combat the Urge to Purchase Unnecessary Clutter 41

    A List of Things to Do 42

Chapter 6: A Minimalist Way Of Life is Good for the Environment 45

    Being Self-Sufficient 45

Streamlining Way Of Life Modifications in a Way That's Good for the Environment 48

Chapter 7: Conserve Your Cash for Larger and Better Things 50

Design a Stunning House With a Couple Of Things 51

Keep in Mind to Stay You and Stay Imaginative! 54

Chapter 8: You Do Not Require a Large House to be Delighted 57

Developing a Budget for Your Minimalistic Way of life 59

Chapter 9: Don't Compare Yourself to Others 62

Cultivating Patience 65

Chapter 10: Delight In a Happier Life as a Minimalist 67

How Minimalism Results In Joy 68

Conserve Time 69

Minimize Stress 69

Increase Freedom 71

Going Deeper 71

Conclusion 75

Thank you for buying this book and I hope that you will find it useful. If you will want to share your thoughts on this book, you can do so by leaving a review on the Amazon page, it helps me out a lot.

Introduction

Nowadays, a lot of us feel as though we do not have all we desire or require. It is all too frequent to feel as though we are without something and to feel that unpleasant sense of yearning, wishing that we had more belongings, or flicking through magazines and living vicariously via others.

Programs like MTV 'Cribs', magazines about interior design, and even YouTube 'room trips' seem to exist to promote this envy and desire and leave us feeling progressively discontented with the important things that we own. This is no accident, as we are going to see.

When life is difficult, and we feel slowed down, we frequently find ourselves believing that if only we had more, we would be more satisfied. The paradox, though, is that this idea could not be further from reality. The truth is that you, in fact, require less to be more pleased.

By embracing a more minimalistic way of life, you can produce more space on your own, own more appealing items and get more satisfaction out of the things you currently have. Believe it or not, you currently have what you need to produce the sort of home set-up that is going to make your family and friends green with envy. You can own a home similar to the ones you have actually been drooling over; however, you do it by doing away with things-- not by getting more!

And what's more, is that when you begin to understand that this mindset is the means forward-- when you begin to get rid of clutter and value the products you own-- you'll discover that you, in fact, end up being much more pleased too.

This book is going to demonstrate to you how to make it take place. You're going to see how to develop a fantastic home that appears as it belongs in a lifestyle magazine while saving time and cash. You'll see how to turn this into a home that accommodates the way of life that you desire and makes your life a lot easier and more pleasurable. And you'll see how to change your attitude into one that enables you to be much more satisfied with the important things you own.

In this book, you are going to discover:

- How to produce a 'zen space' that you can utilize to relax and unwind

- How to take the important things you own and begin using them

- How to arrange clutter and create an arranged, minimal area

- How to alter your attitude to get rid of envy and discover how to value the important things you own genuinely

- How to systemize and automate your life, so you spend less time on routine activities

- How to enormously decrease stress

- How to turn a little home into a high-end pad

- How to spare cash and secure the environment with clever, minimalistic ideas

- Leading pointers for producing a gorgeous minimal décor

- The real meaning behind minimalism and how to embrace its principles

Chapter 1: You Do Not Need to Be Bogged Down with "Stuff."

So just what is a minimalistic way of life? Why is this a lot more than a technique to décor? What does it truly suggest?

" Get all you desire, by finding you currently have it ...".

Basically, a minimalist way of life merely suggests minimizing the clutter, downsizing your belongings, and intending to do more with less. It implies valuing a couple of things rather than having a big quantity of clutter that you do not truly require or desire.

We frequently see minimalism as an approach to UI design for devices from firms like Apple and on an increasing variety of sites. Here, the necessary maxim to follow is 'communicate, do not decorate.' That indicates that unless something is serving a real function, it does not belong in the design.

A site does not require a patterned background, it does not require unneeded menus, and it does not thrive by filling every bit of white area. Every component ought to serve a function, whether that is to direct the viewers' eyes in a specific direction, to communicate some essential information, or to help with a crucial interaction. If a button does not do anything, it does not have to be there!

Bringing Minimal Design Into Your Home

This identical attitude can then be applied to décor. Naturally, you do not have to convey anything as such when it pertains to your home's design, however, you can achieve something comparable when taking a look at items of furnishings, and so on.

Minimalist items of furnishings are products that are practical as they do not have lines or decor that does not have to be there. That suggests that they are going to be comprised of straight lines, and they will not have things like swirly handles, or needlessly fancy feet. It all serves a function.

With that working as the basis for your design, you can then continue with that standard idea by including simply a couple of items that you require while keeping away from the temptation to include additional decor that is going to serve no genuine purpose (naturally we'll be going over how to do all this in following chapters).

In UI and design, this minimalist idea has actually come forward due to the fact that it enables much better interactions. By having less disruptive components, this method has the ability to better direct users to the ideal points on the screen and motivate the appropriate interactions. It additionally permits a site design to better scale to various screen sizes when users use different devices, and it creates more room that makes the experience more relaxing and pleasurable.

However, while your home is not a UI, all these identical principles apply just the same. When you begin getting rid of unneeded decors and clutter, you begin to make engaging with your home much easier. When there are less things on your desk, you'll discover that you can locate what you desire that much more promptly and quickly.

Also, when there is less clutter in your interior decoration, you'll have less clutter in your visual field. This is going to make your area that much more soothing and peaceful and additionally make it a lot easier to keep it orderly.

And that, in turn, implies you're now investing less time cleaning and less time digging around for things. Your house is going to be clean and appealing more frequently, and you'll have more energy and time to do the important things that you take pleasure in doing!

Much like a UI, your home serves a purpose. That purpose is to support the way of life that you wish to live. So, if a thing in your house is not serving that function, then the answer is to remove it! And after that, you can breathe more easily.

Minimalism as a Response to Materialism

A growing number of individuals are beginning to understand the advantages of, in fact, having less clutter and less things and this is leading to a circumstance where they are better off with only a couple of gorgeous items instead of feeling the requirement to head out and purchase all they see promoted on TV.

And what does that cause as a result? Greater fulfillment and joy with less things! This makes a huge distinction since it implies that you're now going to be more pleased and invest less time considering the things that you do not have.

And you'll have more cash to invest in those select couple of products and on the important things that actually make you pleased.

This is the best remedy to our contemporary, materialistic culture, and it is additionally the very same approach that has actually been preached by various philosophies and spiritual practices for centuries. Joy does not originate from what you own. It originates from what you do with what you own.

You could be the wealthiest individual on the planet, yet be extremely stressed out and dissatisfied. Why? Due to the fact that you have actually developed a way of life that still presses the limits of your budget plan. You have actually been accustomed to a particular lifestyle that costs a great deal of cash and includes a great deal of hard work.

Keeping this way of life takes a great deal of effort, and yet you are still constantly considering the things that you do not have and the things you desire. You do not stop to take a minute to take pleasure in the important things you have, and things of unbelievable worth that are already there wind up being lost in all the noise and losing their worth to you.

Minimalism has to do with getting the most out of what you have, and this applies to your private life. Taking an appreciation mindset implies getting up and feeling so fortunate that you're with your partner. It suggests being thrilled with your kids and with your health and with your flexibility. It implies not looking next door and wanting that you had the next-door neighbor's widescreen TV. It suggests not squandering cash on scrap, and it indicates being present.

And naturally, minimalism suggests that your joy isn't bound in physical belongings. It indicates that you can get pleasure out your own mind and your own body, instead of letting that little scratch on your vehicle destroy your day.

Life is there to be indulged in, and there is a lot out there to be savored today. If all you can think about is just how much you desire the most recent toy or gizmo though, then you're not going to have time to stop and take pleasure in those things. You need to work harder, remain in the workplace later, and get loans.

However, what you do not understand is that you currently have all you require. It's time to unwind and enjoy it!

Lots of philosophers concur that this is the secret to joy. To be able to really value things and let go off unneeded tension, sidetracking desires, and that gnawing sense of discontentment.

Obviously, in a capitalist world, where every business under the sun is continuously flaunting its products, this could be extremely tough. Luckily, you have this book to hand, which is going to assist you in getting all you desire by finding that you currently have it.

Chapter 2: The Initial steps to a Minimalistic Way of life

If you resemble many people, then you're most likely living a way of life that is a long way from minimalism. The odds are that each and every single surface area is covered in unnecessary clutter and that you have a lengthy list of things you desire which you plan to spend your cash on and feel like you can't rather pay for the lifestyle that you desire or feel you should have.

You have actually discovered why this is an issue and how it can make you dissatisfied. Now it's time to begin finding a solution for it!

Follow these actions to start your journey towards a genuinely minimalistic way of life.

Decrease Your Clutter

We have actually utilized the word 'clutter' a lot already, and that's due to the fact that it actually is among the most significant issues. Minimalism does not indicate not having wonderful things; it indicates not having the things you do not truly require or desire.

As an experiment, I want you to go into any room in your home and head over to one of the surfaces-- whether that's a bedroom cabinet, a desk or a windowsill. Now, have a look at those objects on display and get rid of 60% of them.

(handwritten note: good idea)

This is going to feel off initially. It is going to feel as though you're removing things you actually like or that you're leaving that surface too sporadic. However, go with it.

What you'll discover is that far from looking worse, getting rid of those things really makes your surface area look a LOT better and that minimalism gives area for your belongings to breathe, and it makes them stand out more. What's more, is that it exposes the real surface beneath and gets rid of the visual 'noise' out of the corner of your eye, which can really wind up producing a great deal of tension.

What's remaining is now the premium 40% of your things. That suggests that what you have actually left behind are going to be things that you truly like. It implies that the typical quality of what's on that surface area is going to increase considerably. And those couple of things that stay are going to state far more about you and are going to bring in a lot more attention-- rather than simply blending into a congested mess.

The very best part, however, is that when you then come to clean up that surface area, you are going to have the ability to do so by merely getting rid of 3 or 4 things, and after that, wiping. This has now ended up being a 3-minute task, rather than a 10-minute task. And picture what is going to occur when you apply that identical reasoning to all the other surface areas in your home!

Now go and do the identical thing for all those other surface areas in your room!

Get rid of Boxes

The reason that getting rid of clutter is so effective is that it offers you psychological space. Our brains are developed to take notice of contrast and things that stick out, and they do this by discharging tiny quantities of stress hormone. The more noise and clutter there is in an area, the more there is for our brains to handle. This could be frustrating, and after a long, tough day at work, it makes it extremely hard to unwind and loosen up.

The reality that they add more work just further imposes the truth that an abundance of things does not contribute to your area.

The identical goes for a variety of other things that you most likely do not recognize are resulting in you being stressed. Case in point: boxes that you have beneath your bed or atop your closet. This most likely appears like a fantastic location for storage that is out of the way and assists you to keep more things. However, the truth is that it is going to create visual clutter and work again.

For starters, boxes underneath the bed and on the closet get terribly dusty unless they have a lid. However, more significantly, they once again are going to occupy your mind by using up space and by getting rid of those important areas of 'space' that make a room feel much larger and much less heavy.

Simply attempt taking the boxes out from under the bed and atop the closet and see if this produces a more peaceful and tidy-looking environment. Do the identical for things atop bookshelves, beneath coffee tables, and crammed behind couches.

And once again, simply think how simpler the cleaning is going to be.

It's time to begin thinking of the negative area in your house as being just as crucial-- if not more crucial-- than the clutter that encompasses it.

Dealing with Cables

Another essential suggestion is to consider your cable management. Today, you most likely have cables running beneath desks, throughout the floor, and almost anywhere else.

Can you guess what these do? That's right: they develop more visual clutter! And they make your house appear a lot messier and chaotic than it most likely is. There are terrific cable management options, which vary from utilizing boxes to save your cables, to connecting them to the underside of desks and the rears of screens. Get imaginative, and you can make a lot more space!

One In, One Out

Among the very best things you may do to keep an uncluttered house is to present guidelines that are going to assist you to keep a more minimalistic design.

One such guideline is 'one in, one out.' This just suggests that each time you purchase a brand-new product, you have to select one you have to do away with. This is going to assist you to keep a reasonable variety of things in your house that never ever become overwhelming, and it is going to assist you to spare cash-- particularly seeing as you can sell the things that you do not require in order to get cash off of the brand-new item. It makes an area for your brand-new thing right away, and it additionally pushes you to think much harder about the important things that you really desire.

This seems like a severe guideline, but once you begin to see and feel the advantages of living a more minimalist way of life, you'll more than happy to do it!

Removing Things

If you follow all of these pointers, then you're going to discover that you're dealing with a great deal of things. This could be an unpleasant procedure; however, there is an art to getting it right.

Initially, you are going to do a huge 'de-clutter' and remove a great deal of things rapidly. This is going to aid you to reset your life so that you have an excellent beginning point to work from.

The primary step is to throw away boxes of things that you have actually been keeping in storage that you never ever utilize. The guideline that is typically provided here is to throw away any box that you have not gone into in the last 3 months (you 'd marvel how many that includes!). Also, get rid of clothing that you have not used in 3 months.

Another idea is to remove these things quickly. If you have items you believe you can get a great deal of cash for, then these are worth selling. However, all else you ought to offer to charity stores or throw away.

It's an error to leave things in bags, to let family and friends go through them, or to attempt and sell every last thing. This not just produces a lot more tension as you need to go through all the things you own (hence implying a great deal of individuals are going to put it off and refrain from doing it!), however, it additionally develops the temptation to reconsider and take things back. This is not the objective of the game!

Chapter 3: Take Pleasure In the Liberty that a Minimalistic Way of life can Offer

Still not persuaded of the worth of going minimalist? Then try moving home!

When you move home, a substantial quantity of clutter and things you do not require is going to make life far tougher! On the other hand, if you can minimize your belongings and clutter down to simply the fundamentals and some things that you actually enjoy, then you'll discover that moving is a million times simpler.

You understand what that implies? It indicates you can truly entertain the concept of moving. And it additionally suggests that you can entertain the concept of putting all your things in storage for some time and going traveling for 3 months. Or how about putting your belongings in the loft and renting your house out to renters while you take a trip?

This is an extremely clear illustration of how having less clutter is really liberating. You now have the freedom to travel the world and make more cash since you have less things! Having a great deal of belongings resembles having a physical anchor keeping you in one location. When you minimize this undesirable mess, you are going to really begin to feel physically lighter!

Producing a Zen Area

Another example of how having less stuff could be liberating, is in the way it is going to enable you to minimize tension.

In lots of ways, our houses are an external reflection of our attitudes. When life is too hectic, and you feel as though it's all getting on top of you, it can lead to a scenario where your house begins to look that way-- you wind up with a mess all over your house that you have not had time to clean. For example, you have washing up accumulating by the sink. Papers are all over, and the little time you get to unwind, you can't take pleasure in since your house is such a mess. Apart from anything else, you need to continuously wrestle with the sensation that there are other things you ought to be carrying out.

How can you get on top of things once again if you can't effectively unwind and loosen up?

Even with the very best effort at going minimal, it is going to take a little time prior to you getting all things simply perfect, and there are going to additionally constantly be times when life gets on top of you once again, and you feel stressed out.

One suggestion then is to produce a 'Zen area.' The concept of this area is that you are going to create one area in your house that is going to be 'sacred.' That indicates that regardless of what else takes place, you are not going to make a mess in this specific room. That, consequently, indicates that you are going to utilize a lot more minimalist style here, and it implies that you're going to make guidelines to keep the area tidy-- like no food and drinks.

The objective is to have one location in your house that is constantly calm, neat and arranged and where you can come and sit with a cup of tea and a book when the world seems to be in turmoil wherever you look.

You Don't Need to Clean as Much!

The next manner in which minimalism gives you freedom is by enabling you to spend a lot less time cleaning. You're then going to take this further again by lowering the quantity of work you have to do to maintain it that way via the procedures and systems.

The majority of us invest a great deal of time carrying out the same couple of activities-- that include things like ironing, washing clothes, washing dishes, and vacuuming. These activities take valuable hours out of our weeks that we might be spending being effective, unwinding or hanging out with our loved ones or buddies.

Going minimal is going to minimize a great deal of this work immediately. Just having less suggests there is less to clean, and you can apply the identical reasoning to other things-- having less clothing is going to indicate you have less to put away and having less crockery is going to result in more area in your kitchen area.

However, you can still go further by introducing numerous systems to automate the work you end up doing. Washing up is something you can automate with a basic dishwashing machine! Lots of people view dishwashing machines as unneeded, however, all of it actually boils down to what you wish to spend your time doing. If you can utilize a dishwashing machine to spend more time with your loved ones or your hobbies, then, undoubtedly, that's an excellent choice!

Also, you can develop sophisticated systems for your paper trays so as to minimize the time you devote arranging documents. You can have a rotor for the clothing you wear so that you devote less time contemplating what you wish to wear on any given day and searching through your closet. And you can waste less time vacuuming by utilizing a robotic vacuum that is going to utilize sensing units to clean your rooms by itself!

Minimalism isn't just about the appearance of your design. It's additionally about producing an area that is going to need very little maintenance and very little work. That can additionally suggest selecting plants that need less upkeep and watering, and it can imply discovering great deals of methods to minimize your workload.

Financial Freedom

Lastly, minimalism can additionally assist you in purchasing yourself a great deal of financial freedom. By having less things that you feel you definitely 'need to own,' you can reduce your routine outgoings and the quantity of cash you depend on to be pleased and satisfied.

The outcome is rather effective. Suddenly, you'll discover that you have less financial stress, less debt, and much less tension because of this.

Our 'wealth' is not ascertained by our revenue alone. Rather, our wealth is ascertained by the difference between the amount we make and the amount we spend. This implies that you can end up being a lot 'better off' and dramatically boost your disposable income, just by decreasing what you spend your cash on.

You have actually seen now that you do not have to keep accumulating more things in order to be delighted and to have an excellent house, so ideally, you'll see that you do not have to spend a fortune on things either.

In addition to purchasing less, keeping in mind to sell items you no longer desire can go a long way to conserving money too. For instance, you may do this by trading in phones-- if you trade up to the next design every generation, then you can, in fact, keep the absolute best and newest phone without needing to spend much cash each time.

Likewise, you can additionally spare a reasonable quantity of cash by decreasing month-to-month outgoings. By considering the important things you wish to spend time doing rather than purchasing things or utilizing your different possessions, you can take pleasure in free activities rather-- like walks in the park or days reading books that you currently own!

Think about 'unplugging' and changing to viewing TELEVISION simply on your laptop!

Discover methods to live more inexpensively by streamlining your life. The outcome is that you'll have the ability to spare heaps of cash, leave debt, and live easily instead of continuously feeling like you're right on the edge of what you can pay for. At the end of the day, this is going to bring far more joy than having a lot of 'things.'

And you can utilize this approach when creating the whole manner in which you wish to live your life. For instance, you may select to purchase a house that is reasonably tinier if that suggests that you can lower your mortgage payments and begin spending more cash on the important things that actually make you delighted.

Chapter 4: Increasing Your Productivity with a Minimalist Way of life

Think about just how much you own that you do not actually utilize or you aren't actually knowledgeable about. Does it result in a minor amount of tension?

Picture the alternative: being totally knowledgeable about precisely what you own and having the ability to go through your mind and do a total 'stock take'. Feels much better, doesn't it?

And really, that sensation goes a long way to making you more energized, less stressed out, and even less productive. You may not recognize it; however, today, there is a great chance that your clutter and lack of organization are making you less efficient!

Obviously, this boils down to developing an excellent home office area that you can work well in. However, it additionally boils down to a great deal of much simpler things. Having a better house, for example, can, in fact, make you very likely to shave, very likely to iron your clothes, and very likely to usually remain on top of things.

On the other hand, needing to dig through drawers whenever you have to locate something or needing to dig through documents to address that essential post is going to just make you less successful in every part of your life.

It's time to take a look at how ending up being more minimal can assist you in producing a lot more efficient workflow.

The Ultimate Office

When it pertains to performance at home, the majority of us are going to consider a home office area where we are most likely to keep a computer system, our crucial files, and most likely any utensils and other products of that nature.

This may be where you do your primary job in the event that you have the luxury of working from home, or it might simply be where you do things like paperwork. Maybe you delight in working on projects here.

However, if you resemble many people, then your workplace is going to be covered in files and documents and look like a bomb has actually struck it. Then there are going to be the wires running across the room.

One method to repair all this is by getting an improved filing system for your files. This can begin with a filing cabinet, and if you aren't able to get one of those for the absence of area, think about a briefcase with a file system. Naturally, some files are very likely to be needed at any given time, and you can't simply file it all away! The remedy to this problem is to utilize paper trays. A great way to arrange these is by thinking in regards to how the human memory functions-- with a 'working,' 'short-term' and 'long term' system.

Your working system is the leading tray, and it's where you place whatever you're dealing with right now. You arrange through this daily, and you either toss things out or place them on the lower draw, which is 'short-term memory.'

Then, at the end of every week on a Friday, you are going to arrange through the short-term tray and place long term products into the filing cabinet, while tossing all else away. This works well since it acknowledges the truth that some things are going to have to be instantly available; however, it additionally pushes you to do your sorting in little pieces instead of letting a mountain of paper accumulate on your desk.

Even better, however, is just to lower the quantity of paper you deal with in general. Having a note pad to keep handwritten notes in is an excellent start, and from there, you ought to additionally check out changing to digital bills and statements when possible. This is going to make it a lot easier to remain arranged, in addition to getting a scanner with OCR (optical character recognition). This is going to let you scan letters and other hardcopy files and turn them into searchable Word files and PDFs. From there, merely shred and discard!

With these things in hand, you'll have the ability to enormously minimize the quantity of paperwork in your workplace and around your home, which is going to make it a lot easier to keep your house neat and to remain efficient.

Cable management is additionally an essential strategy, as we discussed earlier. This can additionally indicate utilizing cordless devices where possible, which is going to provide you with more manners in which you can engage with your technology. You could even utilize items like Amazon Echo, which is going to let you speak to your computer system.

Similarly, attempt to streamline other procedures and things you find yourself frequently doing. Think in regards to efficiency by eliminating the variety of steps required to do any given task. This may imply making sure that you have all the work surface areas you require close-by and quickly accessible, for instance, or it may suggest guaranteeing that the tools you require are simple to take out of a drawer without digging initially!

The secret is to eliminate clutter, however, with the end result of rendering it simpler for you to get work performed. Otherwise, keeping your workplace efficient is going to indicate eliminating things from your surfaces and getting rid of hectic furnishings and patterns.

There's a specific kind of clutter to get rid of from an office too-- which is anything that might be considered as a diversion. The goal is to make certain that you keep your office and your individual life distinct. Your workplace is not meant to be someplace where you enjoy yourself, it is meant to be someplace where you get work done. This is not a location for a second TV and nor is it a location for a lot of books.

This isn't to state that your room ought to be dull-- as a matter of fact, it is usually considered that rooms with a little color and interest are going to be more conducive to performance and creativity particularly. The goal isn't to make a stuffy corporate-looking space in your own home! However, simply ensure that you do keep your space devoid of things that are plainly disruptive, which is going to render it harder for you not to put things off!

Keeping Your Tech Fast and Clean

Keep in mind that just as crucial here is to keep your technology running well. Just as space can end up being an outside representation of your mindset, the identical additionally holds true when it comes to your computer system. If your computer system is covered in desktop icons and if it appears to be taking more and more time to load, then there's a great chance that you have actually been stressed out and slowed down, and this is once again an external illustration of that hectic schedule. Worse, it suggests you'll be most likely to lose crucial files, and it suggests you'll feel more stressed out whenever you turn the computer system on.

Resolve this problem by keeping your computer system as minimal as your space. Make a practice of erasing unneeded icons and files, keep your virus checker current and attempt not to set up things you do not require. The outcome is going to be that your computer system boots quicker and assists you to remain more efficient!

Chapter 5: Include the Crucial Things

The secret to all of this is to have a long, difficult think about what it is you desire from your home and your life and how you can ideally create your design and your set-up to make that achievable.

Frequently, our houses get in the way of what we wish to do and make it tougher for us to be successful and efficient. In fact, our houses ought to be enablers and facilitators that make what we wish to accomplish that a lot easier.

So, where does this inconsistency originate from? Why do so many of us fall short of having congruence in between what we wish to accomplish and the design of our houses?

The response is easy: too many people simply do not understand what we desire, not only from our design, yet additionally from life in general. And once again, marketing and media, generally, are mainly behind this, as we are continuously being shown various ideals and various lifestyles-- and informed that they are the absolute best means for us to enjoy our own lives.

We wind up being drawn in every direction by a hundred various marketing messages and a hundred various wishes. We never ever feel quite pleased with anything, and we're continuously being informed that something else is the secret to joy.

Rather, think about what it is you truly wish to accomplish in life and how you wish to arrive there. If you can do this, then you'll have a straightforward mission statement, and you can then set about creating a home to assist you in achieving that.

Obviously, this may end up being more than a single thing. However, the concept is to understand who you are, what is essential to you, and how you're going to serve that objective.

Turning Your House Into an Asset

For instance, let's state that after a great deal of reflection, you recognize that the things that actually matter to you are your household and your love of music.

This produces a really basic and uncomplicated design. You are going to most likely wish to develop an area where you and your household can hang around together -- maybe a media room where you can all relax on a huge couch and enjoy TV or maybe a huge dining-room where you can take pleasure in large meals together.

And you may additionally create a music area. Or simply embellish your space with things that talk to your love of music.

Now, when making purchasing decisions or considering how to create your space, you ought to constantly stop and ask yourself if it is going to truly assist you to take pleasure in those things more, or if it is going to simply get in the way of them. Is it going to bring you joy truly? Is it going to lead to more work for you, so you, in fact, devote less time to doing the important things you like? Is it going to sidetrack from what you currently have, or take away from it?

With this mindset, you'll no longer be guided by marketing since no marketing is going to be directed at you specifically. You know what your house ought to be and now absolutely nothing ought to have the ability to move you far from that.

How to Combat the Urge to Purchase Unnecessary Clutter

Go through these psychological questions whenever you're thinking about a brand-new purchase and consider how it is going to fit into your way of life every day. Where is it going to go? How is it going to look besides the last thing you acquired?

Simultaneously, attempt to know about the techniques that marketers and even shop managers are going to utilize to attempt to get us to purchase things we do not require. In particular, constantly make certain that you spend some time prior to going to purchase something. The huge bulk of purchases are made based upon a psychological impulse, and this is what can lead us to end up being impulsive. If you go away and think rationally about what you require and what you do not, you'll typically discover you are a lot smarter with your purchases because of this.

Never ever purchase then and there. Constantly have at least one night to sleep on it. The offer is going to still exist in the early morning, regardless of what the marketing might declare!

A List of Things to Do

An effective weapon in the battle versus requiring to keep purchasing brand-new things and an excellent way to practice the principles gone over in this chapter is to create a list of things that you wish to do-- utilizing products you currently have, or without having to purchase anything brand-new.

However the truth is that we frequently forget. The majority of us have a great deal of books on our bookshelf that we have yet to read, games we never

ever finished, and even movies that we have not seen! And nowadays, you can download books free of charge, play games for free and more.

Then there are the activities we never ever appear to have time for that may be our pastimes or simply things that ought to get our lives straight.

And yet, when you get a spare hour, you forget about all these things and wind up simply lying in front of the TV. And when you see something else marketed, you all of a sudden wish to purchase it.

Why are you purchasing a brand-new book, video game or DVD when there is a lot that you currently own that you have yet to utilize? Why are you conserving cash to purchase a huge trendy computer system when you've never ever been out to your neighborhood park?

Having a list of ideas for your night's entertainment can truly alter this. The next time you're bored, you can just examine your list for ideas of things to do. The next time you are lured into purchasing something brand-new, inspect the list and understand that you have plenty to be delighted about without spending more cash or jumbling your house.

Stay concentrated and make a house that assists you with attaining your objective!

Chapter 6: A Minimalist Way Of Life is Good for the Environment

The reasons to go minimalistic go far beyond simply having the ability to produce a much better-looking space while investing less cash! Just as essential, if not more so, is the reality that a minimal way of life can additionally be excellent for the planet.

This begins naturally with the variety of home appliances and gizmos you have actually plugged in at any moment. If you are living a more minimalistic lifestyle and spending a bit less time in front of the TV, for example, then you ought to instantly have a lower energy expense since you'll be spending less on your devices and less on running your house.

Being Self-Sufficient

A principle that is going to frequently appear to go together with being more minimal, is self-sufficiency. The less you require to be pleased, the higher your odds of having the ability to fulfill those requirements yourself. As you live more simply, you can begin to fulfill those needs by yourself, thus freeing yourself much more from the continuous drive of needing to work longer and make more.

There are lots of methods with which you can attain this. One is, obviously, to begin growing your own vegetables and fruits and eating basic meals that do not need anything more. In this manner, you can conserve yourself the time and the cost associated with purchasing a lot from the grocery store, while at the same time assisting you to provide something back to the environment in regards to supporting the regional community and even assisting in fighting some greenhouse gasses by growing your own.

Another example may be to power your house yourself. You can once again do this in a variety of methods. However, changing to a more minimalistic way of life is going to constantly assist as it is going to indicate you require less energy to power the way of life you are living. There are a great deal of choices when it pertains to powering your way of life and minimizing your carbon emissions. One popular alternative is to set up solar panels on your roofing, however, these could be exceptionally costly, include a great deal of work to set up and take a long period of time before they begin paying for themselves.

Rather, think about utilizing a solar generator. It is possible to purchase portable generators for a couple of thousand dollars that could be brought with you, and typically, these are going to even consist of solar panels integrated into them (whereas in other cases, they have to be bought independently). These can typically offer ample power to run a TV, computer system, or perhaps larger products like refrigerators forever. It's a fairly budget-friendly method to begin powering your own way of life without needing to go through a substantial quantity of renovation and spend a fortune.

Other things you may do consist of gathering rainwater, and even recycling things around your home so as to help them go further and to conserve cash instead of continuously purchasing brand-new products.

Streamlining Way Of Life Modifications in a Way That's Good for the Environment

Some other techniques of downsizing are going to do a great deal of good for the environment additionally. These consist of:

- Utilizing the automobile less-- Spend more time in your area to spare cash on fuel and to help in reducing your carbon footprint. Similarly, invest more time walking and biking when you do choose to go out.

- Consume less red meat-- Not just is it pricey; however, it can additionally result in a great deal of waste and a great deal of gases like methane.

- Be a green consumer-- This indicates that you prefer products that are produced in a green and energy-efficient way. By selecting to support these companies, you can assist in sending out a clear message that we wish to see more sustainable approaches utilized by our preferred brand names. What's more, is that this is going to assist you to decrease clutter more (since you're producing a long list of products that you aren't going to purchase), and it is going to assist you in utilizing easier things without unneeded bells and whistles.

Chapter 7: Conserve Your Cash for Larger and Better Things

We have actually gone over a great deal of ways to downsize and live a somewhat more minimal way of life at this point, and ideally, you're beginning to come up with more ideas of your own too.

However, this book isn't about going without, and the goal here is not to downsize so much that you can't do the important things you like to do, and vice versa! Our objective is rather to offer ourselves the ways to develop the type of lifestyle we have actually constantly longed for, but by utilizing what we currently have. It has to do with making that satisfaction nearer, not further!

One method to accomplish this is by conserving our money for the important things that we truly desire and not simply spending everything on things that capture us when we're not looking. Far from having less, we're now having more of what actually matters to us and what can actually make a distinction in our lives.

We have actually currently seen the power of getting rid of things from our surface areas. Now, if we substitute those things with simply a number of things that we actually like and we are truly pleased with and delighted about, we'll have the ability to see and feel the distinction.

And this is how you can develop a high-end home on a reasonably meager budget plan!

Design a Stunning House With a Couple Of Things

You do not need to spend a great deal of cash to have a genuinely sensational house that is going to stick out to individuals. Start by having a clear vision for your house (as we've currently talked about), and that is an excellent start that is going to assist in providing your possessions a cohesive feel and look.

However, what truly makes a house look remarkable when you're visiting it and what is going to make individuals leave from your home thinking 'wow,' is having simply a couple of fantastic stick out features.

When you head into a restroom and see something such as a waterfall walk-in- shower, it can really raise the whole sensation of that area.

Similarly, when you include a water feature, or possibly a fireplace to your garden, this can additionally attract attention in an incredible way and truly make the whole garden stick out as being fantastic. Maybe a smart refrigerator, maybe an indoor 'bubble wall,' or it could be a truly incredible computer set-up.

The secret is to pick things that are going to fit in with the rest of your design, which is going to be 'you.' These have to be things that boost the way of life you have actually picked for yourself.

When you deal with all this, you'll have the ability to construct a house that feels that much more incredible while still being genuine to you. Individuals are going to leave feeling exceptionally envious that you have your own recording studio, or perhaps a wonderful chandelier.

Once again: this is just minimal since you're cutting down on all else. However, that's why it's possible. And it works due to the fact that it supports the way of life you desire and the goals you have actually set on your own.

However, what they are not going to recognize is that you never ever spent more than them-- as a matter of fact, you spent less. That one crucial reason speaks volumes due to the fact that there is less clutter around to diminish it. And you managed it by spending less on the things you didn't require-- and by selling off your other big things.

This has to do with having a vision once again. It has to do with understanding what that thing you desire is and going towards it so that you can arrive and make it happen. As soon as you understand that all you actually desire is a house spa, you can begin cutting down everywhere else.

Keep in Mind to Stay You and Stay Imaginative!

And notice something else about these sensational instances: they are special. Typically it's not about spending the most cash that you potentially can, yet by having a house that is going to be special in some way and show visitors something they have not seen prior. Once again, this originates from staying you and from understanding who you are and what you wish to attain.

I like exercising. That's my thing. And one manner in which I turned my fairly basic and little home gym into something extraordinary and distinct was to purchase gym floor covering to give it that expert appearance, and after that, to utilize LED light strips around the undersides of my gym gear. When I stroll in, I can push a button, and the whole gym shines. This cost me about $50 to establish, and it looks spectacular since it's original. It's common to include colored lighting to a computer system set-up, however, I do think I'm relatively uncommon as somebody who has actually done this for their gym.

Due to that, it's something that sends out all my buddies home green with jealousy!

Another idea is to be imaginative in how you get the important things you desire. You do this by considering the 'root' of what you desire, instead of the product itself. What is it about flat-screen screens that you like? Is it the modernity?

Case in point, if you have actually constantly desired a walk-in closet, however, have not had the ability to pay for one or do not have the area, then ask yourself what it is about that idea that you discover so enticing. Obviously, it's your love of your shoes and clothing and the capability to display them in a really desirable way.

However, you may do that without the walk-in closet, and if you get imaginative and creative, then once again, you can really make this a lot more preferable than it may have been as a walk-in closet.

For instance, what about purchasing a bookshelf, but utilizing that as a cool method to show your shoes and your jewelry? Or how about selecting one wall in your house and getting little racks to stand your shoes on? You can still show the important things you enjoy and get all the wow aspect of that walk-in closet for a portion of the cost while still wowing the heck out of visitors.

However, it's not only about conserving cash so you can purchase other remarkable things. Even better is to move the focus onto your way of life, individuals, and the activities that make you really delighted.

Chapter 8: You Do Not Require a Large House to be Delighted

Obviously, you'll have to draw the line someplace, and all people are going to differ in regards to simply how minimalistic they wish to be. Do you wish to cut down completely and reside in a hut in the wilderness without any TV? Or do you wish to have a couple of high-end products to produce an extraordinary way of life that looks a lot more costly than it is while keeping your upkeep down?

And you additionally want to consider your other costs and where they come in. A minimalist home and way of life may be utilized to support particular visions for your decoration; however, it can additionally be utilized to support a travel lifestyle, of monetary security, or of having the ability to send your kids to the absolute best colleges.

If you understand you love taking a trip, then why bother purchasing a substantial home? Why not purchase a little one-bedroom flat in a location that is budget-friendly, and after that, pump all of that cash into traveling? Having a tinier house can, in fact, force you to live that more minimalist way of life and assist you in maximizing what you have truly.

This is not what the media wants us to think. This is not what huge enterprises want us to find. It's not even what the political leaders want us to understand.

As we have actually mentioned already, contemporary culture is tailored towards producing things that individuals desire (yet do not require) in order to provide us with an inspiration to keep working harder and harder. The paradox is that in fact being in good shape and warm can cost a small amount.

If you head to the appropriate part of the nation and purchase a property that is little enough, you can possibly totally pay off a mortgage in a handful of years.

Integrate that with a minimalist way of life, some self-sufficiency, and in a couple of years' time, you'll have all the important things you have actually ever desired while spending hardly a couple of hundred dollars a month on your living expenses. You'll never ever deal with debt once again, and if you can discover a method to make simply a small amount of cash online, then you can even leave the 9-5 life behind.

Developing a Budget for Your Minimalistic Way of life

Once again, it boils down to having that vision so you understand what it is you wish to do. However, you do not only require a vision-- you additionally require a strategy so that you can set about enacting it and, in fact, turning it into a reality.

We do this by producing a budget plan. This budget plan ought to consist of all of your earnings and all of your outgoings and you'll wish to put this into a spreadsheet. You ought to have the ability to utilize this information to develop a visualization of your financial resources and even to utilize 'financial modeling' to see if you have a rising or falling pattern.

Then what you're going to do is to take a look at just how much cash you have remaining at the end of a given week or month and just how much cash you can conserve or choose to spend on other things you desire.

And from here, you can then utilize your chart to see how long it is going to take for you to make X quantity of cash.

Keep your vision plainly in mind, whether that is taking a trip around the world or constructing that house spa. Know precisely just how much it is going to cost and utilizing your forecasts; precisely how long it is going to take you to generate that much cash.

And now, begin considering methods to reduce that time frame. This may indicate that you begin cutting down on the important things you do not truly require. It may indicate selling a couple of unneeded products. It may imply minimizing your outgoings by purchasing less things you do not require.

See how you are naturally beginning to produce an increasingly more minimalistic way of life. However, it is going to feel worth it now since you have that incredible vision in mind at the end of it.

And in the meantime, keep in mind that you ought to have that list of excellent activities to do at nights and at weekends to assist you in living that minimal way of life. You do not have to keep spending cash on Netflix and on scrap when you're spending your weekends exploring your area composing books or doing things that are simply far more satisfying.

Ideally, you're additionally now spending more time with friends and family-- which is additionally free of cost-- and seeing yourself move inexorably in the direction of your objectives.

Chapter 9: Don't Compare Yourself to Others

When talking about methods in which you can design a fantastic home inexpensively, we have actually pointed out a number of times when this is going to make your buddies and visitors quite jealous. This is something we have actually been concentrating on for a great reason-- due to the fact that it's most likely what is a huge driving force for you when purchasing things.

It is human nature to desire what other individuals have and to be continuously looking over the fence at the next-door neighbors' brand-new automobile and wanting it. This is really a driving force that makes us a lot more efficient, and in the wild, it would have assisted us in keeping progressing and making ourselves better partners with higher status.

In today's world however-- where we no more have to end up being alpha male and female-- all this does is make us a lot less delighted.

And this isn't simply something you read on automobile bumper stickers. This is a scientific truth based upon actual psychological research studies. In the event you require evidence: it even has its own name, which is is 'social comparison theory,' and it generally claims that a great deal of our joy and sense of achievement originates from comparing ourselves to others.

In these research studies, psychologists have actually examined the joy of individuals with various incomes. What they discovered was that it didn't matter a lot just how much the individual was making-- yet just how much they were making compared to their peers.

To put it simply, if you were making $100,000 a week, you may still not be happy if your buddies were all making $200,000 a week. This social contrast is what you utilize as your barometer and due to the fact that you're making less, you feel disappointed-- despite the fact that you can pay for all of the important things you desire and do all the things you desire.

Alternatively, however, if you were making $100 a week and everybody else was making $5 a week, then you would likely be much more pleased!

Social contrast is believed to be among the leading reasons for civil unrest, criminal activity and unhappiness. And it is something that a great deal of us wrestle with. The most awful part of all this? Today we are no longer contrasting ourselves to individuals who we live beside or who we work with. And we are no longer comparing ourselves to our buddies.

Rather, we're comparing ourselves to stars. To individuals in publications who appear to be able to pay for the largest houses you can possibly imagine and to those previously mentioned YouTubers. How can we actually be pleased when we're continuously being shown such incredible things?

Once again, the response is to stop comparing yourself and to stop desiring things for the sake of it. Stop desiring things since you don't have them and, rather, begin to feel gratitude and satisfaction for the important things that you do have. Once again, it implies thinking of what you desire from life, who you are, and how you're going to get those things you desire. It implies having a vision.

When you do so, then you no longer have to compare yourself to those individuals due to the fact that now you understand that what makes them delighted isn't what makes you delighted. That product may not, in fact, improve your life and assist you in reaching your objectives-- it may well produce more work and get in the way of what makes you happiest!

This can call for a cognitive shift once you recognize that it truly does not matter what Jeff next door has, you'll discover it leads not just to higher levels of joy yet likewise to much better satisfaction and smarter life choices. You'll invest your cash more carefully, and you'll normally be a greater and more pleased version of yourself!

Cultivating Patience

Another crucial cognitive shift to utilize here is to accept patience. Really frequently, we wind up getting ourselves into debt, wasting more cash than we have, and filling our houses with clutter not due to the fact that we desire so much, but since we desire it right now.

We'll make excuses for ourselves to purchase things right now like: 'it may not be here if I don't purchase it now' or 'I'll get the cash back next week.' The truth? If you purchase the product before you have the cash now, you'll be very likely to do the very same thing following week.

This has to do with discipline, and it has to do with understanding what you desire and waiting to get it. That's what is going to permit you to get the important things you desire without tension and without debt, and it's what is going to keep your house from being filled with increasingly more unneeded products. And this actually reinforces the value of being selective.

Chapter 10: Delight In a Happier Life as a Minimalist

We have actually seen how embracing a more minimalist way of life can assist you to:

- Conserve cash

- Be more efficient

- Assist the environment

- Design a far more lovely home

- Support the way of life that actually makes you delighted

- Leave the rat race

All those are quite worthwhile causes. And regardless of what sort of individual you are, merely decreasing the clutter in your house and altering the manner in which you think about your purchases are going to assist you to be a more satisfied version of that individual.

However, none of that is the supreme objective of this book. The genuine objective rather is to make you better and happier.

How Minimalism Results In Joy

There are 2 manners in which minimalism results in joy: direct and indirect.

We're going to take a look at how you can utilize minimalism to actually change your frame of mind and your relationship with your possessions; however, we are going to come to that in a moment.

Meanwhile, what we're interested in is a few of the direct repercussions of minimalism and how that makes you more pleased.

We have actually discussed these things already; however, to summarize, going minimal is going to assist you to:

Conserve Time

You have far less clutter in your house now, which implies you have less cleaning to do. You have actually introduced easy systems to assist you to wash up and keep your home tidy, and you are less demanding on yourself.

All this suggests that you can now get home and, in fact, unwind in a calm and good-looking environment. It's impossible to overemphasize simply what a favorable effect this can have on your life or just how much of an improvement this can make.

Minimize Stress

You live a cheaper lifestyle, and therefore, you can really work less. When you understand that you can attain all those things you wish to attain without remaining in work up until 8 pm and without taking on a great deal of additional responsibility and overtime, then you understand that you do not have to work more to be happier!

Now you're getting home earlier and not delivering that tension home with you. That makes you a far better buddy, a far better spouse, and a far better parent.

What about job fulfillment, you ask? Well, maybe you want to stop taking a look at your work as a way to attain your fulfillment. What about acquiring fulfillment from your own undertakings rather? How about writing a fantastic novel, getting into amazing shape, or going on fantastic journeys?

What about establishing an extremely fulfilling side business? Or working online?

On the other hand, you additionally have less work to do around your home and less monetary stress. If the boiler breaks, you will not have a fit recognizing that you can't pay for it since you have lots of disposable income!

There's no debt, no threat of not making your next mortgage payment. The less you understand what you require, the more relaxed and exciting life ends up being once again!

Increase Freedom

Less tension and less physical ties lead to more freedom. You do not have to stress over your home being robbed while you're away, and you do not have to stress over bringing lots of things with you if you pick to move house. When you have more area in your house, you have more freedom simply to move around in that area!

Freedom is such a basic aspect of the human experience and definitely vital to our joy!

Going Deeper

However, that joy goes much deeper. Due to the fact that minimalism is actually about understanding that you have all you require to be delighted right here, today. Leave that hedonic treadmill and acknowledge that fact, and you can begin to value how fortunate you are, and you can start being delighted with anything.

However, if you constantly feel you desire more and if you're constantly pressing towards that next thing, then you'll discover you never ever truly stop to take pleasure in the important things you currently have. Stop this by establishing a gratitude mindset.

An excellent way to do this is to spend every evening analyzing all you have and all you're thankful for, for simply 5 minutes. This may imply writing those things down in a note pad, or it can suggest going through them mentally.

Attempt to think about various things every night. And there is a lot to be grateful for. You could be grateful for the reality you are in good health. You could be grateful for the truth that you have individuals who love you. And you could be grateful for the truth that you have a roof over your head whatsoever.

Another idea is to make certain you arrange the time to take pleasure in the important things you own and the area you have. Even better, ensure that you are really delighting in the important things that you are doing too. We have our list of things that we may do for an evening, and this could be a variety of things from stargazing in your own garden to constructing a robot with the children.

Whatever the case, attempt to be imaginative when composing this list and to consider all the various manners in which you can utilize the area you currently have to have a good time. Take a look at things you have around you and attempt to think about the brand-new and amazing ways in which you might have a good time with them or do something rewarding or satisfying. Attempt to discover that kid's sense of marvel in your own home.

However, what's more, is that you then have to make an effort to truly review what you're doing and how lucky you are. This is referred to as being 'present' or being 'mindful,' and it is presently a huge subject in psychology. It basically indicates that rather than letting your mind think about work and all the important things you're worried about today, you're rather going to stop and assess what you're doing and just how much fun you're having. When you're being in your conservatory or orangery, take a minute to think how excellent it is to be able to observe the stars outside as you sit warm inside your home.

Discover how it actually does not matter what you have. What matters is your viewpoint of the important things you have. What matters is your gratitude. You produce value in the manner you engage with the world and your possessions, and in carrying this out, you bring worth into your own life. You could be abundant without spending a cent.

Conclusion

Ideally, this book has actually offered you a thorough summary of the subject of minimalism, and ideally, it has actually demonstrated to you how it can enhance your life on a great deal of various levels.

This is a book about getting rid of the clutter and getting rid of the tension in your life so that you can begin delighting in the important things that matter to you more. It has to do with understanding precisely what you desire in life and pursuing it.

It has to do with house decoration and producing the remarkable pad that you constantly desired without investing a fortune and putting yourself in dreadful debt.

Ideally, it has actually motivated you to turn your house into something a lot more elegant while cutting your clutter in half, minimizing the quantity of cash you're spending, and having to work less. Possibly you have some ingenious ideas for decoration that are going to be distinct to you, which are going to look a lot more costly than they are!

However it's additionally about making that cognitive shift. It has to do with acknowledging that you do not require a great deal of things to be delighted and that actually, all that stuff is most likely making you much less pleased. It's most likely making you worried, it's most likely stopping you from doing things you wish to do, and it most likely costs you a great deal of cash.

Furthermore, you most likely never ever actually desired it in the first place. You were most likely fooled into feeling like you desired it by smart marketing and our business culture.

Rather then, it's time to reclaim control. It's time to develop a strategy and a vision for what you desire, and after that, to just spend cash and fill your home when you can really support the way of life you wish to live.

And when you get out of that vicious cycle of desiring more and valuing less, you'll discover it can result in a transformative cognitive shift that assists you to be much more pleased and more satisfied.

It's an incredible journey, and it starts with removing a couple of things you do not require anymore. Take that initial step today!

I hope that you enjoyed reading through this book and that you have found it useful. If you want to share your thoughts on this book, you can do so by leaving a review on the Amazon page. Have a great rest of the day.

Printed in Great Britain
by Amazon